MY PERSONAL
Pet Remembrance
J O U R N A L

By Enid Samuel Traisman, M.S.W.

A
Dove Lewis Emergency Animal Hospital
Resource

©1996 ENID SAMUEL TRAISMAN PORTLAND, OREGON

ISBN #0-9651131-0-8

A Gift From:

FOREWORD

Shakespeare, in his play *Much Ado About Nothing*, points out that "Any person can manage grief, but he who has it". None of us know what the "right" way to grieve is, yet we all engage in this process when a significant attachment is disrupted by loss. Enid Traisman, MSW, has added a new tool that can be used to get through the bereavement, mourning, and grief following the loss of a pet. That pets are significant in many of our lives is non-refutable. They offer us protection, companionship, humor, and unconditional love. The loss of a pet is experienced by many in ways analogous to loss of a human significant other and in many cases to an even greater level. *My Personal Pet Remembrance Journal* is a sensitive, thorough, effective adjunct in assisting those going through pet loss related grief. The book reminds us what normal grief is about and how not to be ashamed of those feelings. It provides opportunities for nostalgic memories that we know are so important in the mastering of grief. The book provides an opportunity to memorialize, remember, and to move on when ready. This book is mandatory for those going through this extremely difficult time in their lives. Children, adolescents, and adults of all ages will benefit from Ms. Traisman's treatment and insight into pet loss.

Herbert Nieburg, Ph.D.
Author- *Pet Loss: A Thoughtful Guide for Adults and Children* Four Winds Hospital- Katonah, N.Y.(Harper-Collins)

$\mathcal{T}$his Remembrance Journal is especially for you. It is a special place for you to share the feelings that have arisen since the death of your beloved pet. Here you can write down your thoughts and feelings that are ever-present and ever-changing. In your journal you can privately go over the details of your loss and its effect on you.

Your reaction to the death of your pet is as unique and individual as was your relationship. Your personal grief reaction is affected by your experience with previous losses, how closely bonded you were to your pet, cause of death, support system and your personal nature. My hope is that this guided journal will help you as you move along the challenging journey ahead of you.

There are no shortcuts or specific steps to follow to make grieving quicker or less painful. The strength of the bond you had with your pet often serves as a barometer for the intensity of the grief you feel. Experiencing the pain of your loss is an essential part of working through and integrating your grief. You never forget - You received a lot from your pet and will always have in your heart the love he/she gave to you.

Know that there is no perfect way to grieve. There is no wrong way to use your journal. It is here for you to express your thoughts and feelings. You can use it to help you experience, explore and understand the emotional roller coaster you are on. You do not have to complete every sentence or fill every space. Use only those that feel right for you. Sometimes you will have a lot to write, other times you may just want to read and think. Write in any area that touches your heart at the moment, even if it is in the middle or end of the journal. Be creative, use colored pens and markers, glue in pictures and meaningful clippings. Personalize your journal so that it intimately reflects you and your pet and all that you shared. *Enid*

*O*UR ANIMALS

SHEPHERD US

THROUGH CERTAIN ERAS

OF OUR LIVES.

WHEN WE ARE READY

TO TURN THE CORNER

AND MAKE IT

ON OUR OWN...

THEY

LET US GO.

AUTHOR UNKNOWN

NORMAL GRIEF RESPONSE AFTER THE DEATH OF YOUR PET

Reasons why it may hurt so much when a pet dies
- Your pet is a source of unconditional love and appreciation
- A pet becomes part of who you are; an alter-ego, child and/or companion
- Many times, places, feelings, thoughts and events are associated with your pet
- Your pet did things just for you and you did things just for your pet
- Each of you gave the other a great deal of emotional support
- Losing your pet is like losing a part of yourself

What you might feel after the death
- Shock/numbness
- Denial
- Anger/guilt
- Regret
- Relief
- Depression

What you may experience physically
- Crying
- Dry mouth, difficulty in swallowing
- No appetite or over-eating
- Sleep disturbances
- Aching heart, chest pains and/or an empty, hollow feeling
- Lack of energy and motivation
- Unable to concentrate, forgetfulness
- Sensitivity to loud noises

What you may experience emotionally
- Everything reminds you of your pet, you may experience seeing or hearing your pet
- Feeling distanced from others, as if no one understands or cares
- Questioning the meaning of life and mortality, re-evaluating your priorities in life
- Worrying about others you love dying
- Afraid to love again, fear of the pain of loss

The labor of mourning
It is called the labor of mourning because it is exhausting and difficult work to grieve over the loss of a loved one. The "work" is actually feeling the pain that you experience whenever you think of or are reminded of your pet who is no longer with you. Healthy grieving is going through the pain. It is a typical response to try avoiding the pain. In the long run that may make things worse. The pain of the loss will soften in time if you acknowledge it. Yes, pain hurts and it is uncomfortable, but it is not bad; it is a testimony of the love and joy you shared with your pet.

What helps soften the pain
- Talking, talking... To family, friends, co-workers, a support group and/or counselor
- Writing about your pet and about your feelings in a journal
- Creating a funeral /memorial service, sharing memories, sharing your pain
- Be extra kind to yourself; get a massage, a bubble bath, exercise, visit with friends
- Set up a memorial in your pet's honor.
- Create a ritual repeat it every year

©1995 Enid S. Traisman, M.S.W. Enid is a Grief Counselor and the author of three self help, fill-in journals for people who have suffered the death of a loved one; I Remember, I Remember... A Keepsake Journal for Adults, Fire in My Heart, Ice in My Veins A Journal for Teenagers Experiencing a Loss and a Child Remembers published by The Centering Corporation, Omaha, NE (402) 553-1200.

THIS JOURNAL IS IN LOVING REMEMBRANCE OF:

Date of Arrival:

Date of Death:

Journal Keeper:

This keepsake journal is a record of important facts,
special thoughts and warmest memories.
The purpose of this book is to enhance your healing
process and honor your relationship with your pet.

PHOTOS

OUR BEGINNINGS

The Date: _____

The City and State: _____

The whole story of how, when and where we first met each other.
Describe the circumstances, your feelings, reactions, intuitions, and first
impressions.

_____

_____

_____

_____

_____

_____

_____

_____

_____

_____

_____

_____

_____

_____

What I know about your personal history:
What breed(s) were your parents, were you planned, how many in your litter, did you come from a breeder, shelter, pet shop or other?

What you looked like, felt like, smelled like when I first got to be with you:

Unique and notable personality traits you showed from the beginning:

_____

_____

_____

_____

_____

We Named You
How long it took to come up with your name. Other ideas we had. Why this is the name we chose and how it fit your looks and/or personality.

_____

_____

_____

_____

_____

Nicknames and Endearments:

_____

_____

_____

_____

_____

_____

PHOTOS

YOUR PERSONAL SPACE AND BELONGINGS

Color of your collar, tags and leash:

_____
_____
_____
_____
_____

What your ID tag said:

_____
_____
_____
_____
_____

Favorite appropriate toys:

_____
_____
_____
_____
_____

Favorite inappropriate toys:

_____
_____
_____
_____
_____

Favorite treats:

_____

Where you slept/ where you were supposed to sleep:

_____

Any unusual or specific preferences:

_____

LOOKING BACK AT THE EARLY YEARS

Fill pages with funny, cute and memorable stories and pictures:

AS OUR LIVES AND ROUTINES EVOLVED

What your typical day was like:

_____

_____

_____

_____

_____

_____

_____

_____

_____

The greeting you gave me when I would return home:

_____

_____

_____

_____

_____

_____

_____

_____

_____

_____

_____

What we enjoyed doing together most was:

Places we loved to walk:

People and animals we loved visiting with:

_____

_____

_____

_____

_____

_____

_____

_____

_____

Comments people would make about you:

_____

_____

_____

_____

_____

_____

_____

_____

_____

_____

_____

This is how you let me know what you wanted:

_____
_____
_____
_____
_____
_____
_____
_____
_____

Favorite games we played:

_____
_____
_____
_____
_____
_____
_____
_____
_____
_____
_____

Tricks I taught you to do, and tricks you taught me to do:

_____

_____

_____

_____

_____

_____

Some things that you did not like at all:

_____

_____

_____

_____

_____

_____

Mischievous things you did and why:

_____

_____

_____

_____

_____

_____

Vacations we took together and how we got there:

_____

_____

_____

_____

_____

_____

_____

_____

_____

_____

_____

_____

_____

_____

_____

_____

_____

_____

Who took care of you when I went away and how you liked it:

_____

_____

_____

_____

_____

How we celebrated Holidays:

_____

_____

_____

_____

_____

_____

_____

_____

_____

_____

_____

_____

_____

_____

_____

_____

_____

_____

_____

_____

_____

_____

PHOTOS

OUR SPECIAL BOND

All that we've shared is woven in my heart.
Each thread is a memory
From which I will never part

Ways that we were especially close:
Include emotional, physical, intuitive, psychic, companionship, therapeutic...

_____
_____
_____
_____
_____
_____
_____
_____
_____
_____
_____
_____
_____
_____
_____
_____
_____
_____
_____
_____
_____
_____
_____
_____
_____

In so many ways you met my needs:

You were by my side during these major life events, joyful and painful:

Special things that I did for you as expressions of my love and gratitude:

SPECIAL KEEPSAKES

MEDICAL HISTORY

What you thought of your Veterinarian, examinations and shots:

_____

_____

_____

_____

_____

What I thought of your Veterinarian:

_____

_____

_____

_____

_____

Document important medical information here:

_____

_____

_____

_____

_____

_____

_____

_____

THE END OF YOUR LIFE

Here is a description of the last weeks and days of your life as I can now recall them:

Special "last time" events that we shared:

Difficult decisions I made and why:

Why I was or was not with you when you died, and what it was like:

Why I chose to see you/be with your body after your death, or why I chose not to and how I feel about it:

If I could rewrite the end of your life, it would be:

DISPOSITION OF YOUR REMAINS

I had to choose between letting our Veterinarian take care of your remains, burial or cremation.   This is what I chose and why:

Special items placed with your body. Describe their significance and symbolism:

Your final resting place is:

This place was chosen because:

Others who were with me to do a service for you, or why I was alone:

Special things I said or did, or wish I had:

Choices I've made, or have not made about your personal belongings:

These items I will keep and cherish forever:

THE LABOR OF MOURNING

My pain over the loss of you is sometimes physical, this is how I feel it:

These are the painful emotions that drain me:

The times of day that are regularly hard for me are:

These things I cannot bear to do since your death:

Late at night, when the world is fast asleep, I am awake thinking about:

This is what is most difficult about coming home:

_____

_____

_____

_____

_____

_____

_____

_____

_____

This is what is comforting about being home:

_____

_____

_____

_____

_____

_____

_____

_____

_____

_____

_____

_____

There have been jolting reminders of your death:

There are times when I have an unexpected stab of pain:

There are times when I feel unexpected happiness:

_____

_____

_____

_____

_____

_____

_____

_____

_____

_____

There are times I think I hear you, see you, or feel your presence. This is how I interpret and feel about this phenomenon:

_____

_____

_____

_____

_____

_____

_____

_____

_____

_____

What I miss most about you right now:

REGRETS

I can't help but thinking; "If only" and "Why did I" or "Why didn't I".
Things I regret and feel guilty about:

_____

_____

_____

_____

_____

_____

_____

_____

_____

_____

_____

_____

_____

_____

_____

_____

_____

_____

_____

_____

_____

_____

_____

What I am sorry for:

In my heart I know that I would never intentionally have harmed you. I know I must forgive myself as you would forgive me. This is what I am doing to work toward forgiving myself so that I can lessen my grief and continue to heal:

PREVIOUS LOSSES
"New grief awakens the old" Thomas Fuller

Other losses I have experienced and when those losses occurred:

_____

_____

_____

_____

_____

_____

My feelings at the time and how I coped:

_____

_____

_____

_____

_____

_____

How my feelings are different and similar over the loss of you:

_____

_____

_____

_____

_____

_____

PHOTOS

LEARNING TO GRIEVE IN A HEALTHY WAY

You don't heal from a loss because time passes, you heal because of what you do with the time.

Here is a list of healthy ways I can work through my pain:

People I can talk to:

Places I feel comfortable crying:

Ways of pampering myself:

Creative expressions of my love and loss:

I am learning to accept that grief affects all areas of my life. I can't do everything as well as I did before. Give examples for:

Inability to concentrate:

Lack of motivation:

Low energy level:

Lack of focus:

Sleep patterns are disturbed, this is what I am doing to ensure I get enough sleep:

Eating patterns are different, this is what I am doing to keep my diet healthy:

Physical activity helps release endorphins, natural healing agents. This is the exercise routine I am trying to do to keep my body healthy during this stressful, painful time:

I am learning to recognize when I am avoiding facing my pain. These are the signals I get:

GRIEF SHARED IS GRIEF DIMINISHED

If someone listens, or stretches out a hand, or whispers a kind word of encouragement, or attempts to understand a lonely person, extraordinary things begin to happen.
— Shared at a support group

My experiences talking to family:

Talking to friends:

Journaling:

Attending a Pet Loss support group:

THE RAINBOW BRIDGE

There is a bridge connecting Heaven and Earth. It is called The Rainbow Bridge because of its many colors. Just this side of The Rainbow Bridge there is a land of meadows, hills, and valleys with lush green grass.

When a beloved pet dies, the pet goes to this place. There is always food, water, and warm spring weather. The old and frail animals are young again. Those who were maimed are made whole again. They play all day with each other.

There is only one thing missing. They are not with their special person who loved them on Earth.

So each day they run and play until the day comes when one suddenly stops playing and looks up. The nose twitches! The ears are up! The eyes are staring! And this one suddenly runs from the group!

You have been seen, and when you and your special friend meet, you take him or her in your arms and embrace. Your face is kissed again and again and again, and you look once more into the eyes of your trusting friend. Then you cross The Rainbow Bridge together, never again to be separated...

Author Unknown

DREAMS

My dreams about you:

_____

_____

_____

_____

_____

_____

_____

_____

_____

FAITH AND SPIRITUALITY

Life is faith, whether we recognize it or not

My beliefs about being reunited are:

_____

_____

_____

_____

_____

_____

_____

_____

MEMORIALIZING
Creating special ways of remembering your pet

This is what is inscribed in my heart and on your final resting place:

In your memory donations have been and will be made to:

In your memory I have developed the following rituals which help me feel close to you:

To recognize your absence and keep your memory alive during special holidays and/or anniversaries I will:

I CAN FEEL MYSELF HEALING

I first thought of you with happiness and not pain when:

I first laughed and felt good when:

I made a conscious decision to triumph over my grief when:

I can look at your picture, have a memory and visit a special place sometimes without crying:

PHOTOS

I HAVE GROWN FROM THIS EXPERIENCE

Although death is an ending, it is also a beginning.
Death has much to teach us about living.

What I have learned about myself since your death:

_____
_____
_____
_____
_____
_____
_____
_____
_____
_____
_____

How my priorities in life have changed:

_____
_____
_____
_____
_____
_____
_____
_____
_____
_____
_____
_____
_____
_____
_____
_____

Things I was never aware of before but am now:

I now recognize these strengths in myself that were previously untapped:

Changes I am making in my life as a result of loving you and grieving over your death:

FINAL GIFTS

What did your pet find most lovable about you?

_____

_____

_____

Which of these "gifts" did you receive as a result of having such a special relationship with your pet?

To love unconditionally _____

To be more accepting of yourself _____

To be true to yourself in times of crisis and doubt _____

Wisdom _____

Courage _____

Forgiveness _____

Spontaneity _____

To give yourself over to love _____

To be open to joy _____

To communicate love _____

To grow in humility _____

Find some way to thank your pet for parting gifts they left.

MY GOOD-BYE LETTER

SPECIAL PHOTOS

SPECIAL PHOTOS

SPECIAL KEEPSAKES

SPECIAL KEEPSAKES

RECOMMENDED BOOKS ON PET BEREAVEMENT

The following books can be found at your library, bookstores, the publishers, or Direct Book Services at (800) 776-2665.

Animals As Teachers and Healers by Susan Chernak McElroy (Published by Sage Press, Portland, Oregon, 1996)

Coping with the Loss of a Pet by Christina M. Lemiux, Ph.D. (Reading, PA: Wallace Clark Publishers, 1992).

Between Pets and People by Alan Beck, Sc.D., and Aaron Katcher, M.D. (New York: Putnam, 1983).

Dog Heaven by Cynthia Rylant(Scolastic Inc., 555 Broadway, New York, NY 10012-3999)

Good-bye My Friend, Grieving the Loss of a Pet by Mary and Herb Montgomery (Minneapolis, MN: Montgomery Press, 1994)

Pet Loss: A Thoughtful Guide for Adults and Children by Herbert A. Nieburg and Arlene Fisher (New York: Harper & Row, 1982).

Especially for children
The Tenth Good Thing About Barney by Judith Viorst (New York: Antheneum, 1975).

Goodbye, Mitch by Ruth Wallace-Brodeur (Morton Grove, IL: Alber Whitman & Co. 1995).

It Must Hurt A Lot A child's book about death by Doris Sanford (Milwaukie, OR: Multnomah Press, 1985).

LIFETIMES: The beautiful way to explain death to children by Mellonie & Ingpen (New York: Bantam Books, 1983).

Recommended by Enid Traisman, M.S.W. and The Dove Lewis Emergency Animal Hospital, Portland, Oregon who provide free Pet Loss Support Groups four times each month. Call for a brochure and more information at (503) 228-7282.

FOR MORE COPIES OF THIS BOOK

My Personal Pet Remembrance Journal

For copies of ten or less, order through:
Direct Book Service

Retail price $9.95 each
Shipping & Handling extra

Credit card orders: 1-800-776-2665
FAX Orders: 1-509-662-7233
Internet: *dgctbook@cascade.net*
Compuserve   75027,3255
Mail Orders: **Direct Book Services**
                        P.O. Box 2778
                        Wenatchee, WA 98807

For quantity orders and discounts, contact: Enid Traisman @ 1-503-234-2061
Or write:

Enid Traisman, M.S.W.
3957 NE Couch St.
Portland, Oregon 97232

☐ I have enclosed $ (check or money order only), payable to DLEAH Publications

☐ Please charge my Visa/Mastercard account (circle One)

Card Number

Expiration Date

Signature

Name

Address

City   State   Zip

Phone

☐ Please send my purchase as a gift to

To:

Address

City   State   Zip

Phone

From:

Please note that prices are subject to change without notice.
This form may be photocopied for multiple uses.
For more information, bulk sales or additional forms, please call 1-503-234-2061

ABOUT THE AUTHOR

Enid Samuel Traisman, MSW is a therapist specializing in bereavement and loss in Portland, Oregon. She is a devoted mother to her human children, Noah and Maya, and to her large (and ever increasing) menagerie of critters who surround her with buoyant spirits and unconditional love. Enid operates a private therapy practice and presents seminars to care givers and to grieving people. In 1986, Enid founded Dove Lewis Emergency Animal Hospital Pet Loss Support Group. She continues to facilitate those groups today. Enid authored three fill-in journals for human loss published by The Centering Corporation.